Pigeons and…

Also by William Minor

tree on the outside (Coracle Press)

William Minor

Pigeons and Pussy

Shearsman Books

First published in the United Kingdom in 2013 by
Shearsman Books
50 Westons Hill Drive
Emersons Green
BRISTOL
BS16 7DF

www.shearsman.com

ISBN 978-1-84861-307-2

PIGEONS

Pussy

Pigeons have no respect for
the institution of the language of men
and men have no respect for
the institution of the image of pigeons.

Pussy is not rooted in the world of prose
it is rooted in the world of pussy. The poetry
of pussy is in the presentation of pussy.

A man cannot stand
in the center of pigeons
without standing in
the center of something
that has never even seen a pigeon.

I like pussy
up real close
where all I can
see is the pussy.

Even when speaking of alien things,
a poet speaks his own language, which is
the language of pigeons.

Some pussy establishes a link
between one continuous block of pussy
and one that appears quite briefly.

An incomprehensible exchange
between two images is an exchange
between an image of two pigeons.

Pussy is a labyrinth of paths. You approach from one side and you know your way about; you approach the same place from another side and no longer know your way about.

The man standing and staring at the pigeons
will soon be standing and staring at the sudden loss
of pigeons, followed by the sudden loss of standing and
staring at the loss of pigeons.

If we are to speak of the great pussy,
let us speak of the eternity of the pussy
and the generality of the pussy before we
begin speaking of any specific pussy.

What does a woman have for a head
if what a pigeon has for a head is a head.

Through the window you could see all of the usual props of reality suspended in their usual spots. The usual spot for pussy is on the woman who has the pussy.

Pigeons can be
very expressive
when faced with
an oppressing force
that is not a pigeon.

The reality is
that pussy belongs
somewhere that strikes
the poet as ordinary.

If we use
a normal pigeon
as an example,
other pigeons may
lead to boredom.

When the human mind is
put to the problem of pussy
it is put through the test of being
completely enveloped by pussy.

The world of the woman who feeds the pigeon
is the world in which the image of the pigeon has not
been torn down.

The formal properties of pussy
do not impoverish its metaphysical content.

Some pigeons appear much larger
in reality than they do in dreams in which
reality plays no part in the appearance of pigeons.

Sometimes pussy disappears
only to reappear in the form of
an evening spent without pussy.

The man who left something
for the pigeons left them an image
of a man who does not like pigeons.

I have never maintained visual indifference
in the presence of pussy. Between a shovel, a shoe,
a door and a pussy, I find my eye always falls
on pussy. Once the eye falls on pussy it falls away
from everything that is not pussy.

Some pigeons have
the legs to go forward
and some women have
ordinary pigeons to feed.

Pussy
usually
appears
with
exemplary
clarity.

Men who die
for beautiful ideas
do not bring freedom
to pigeons.

It seems clear to me
the pussy emanates from
an inaccessible source which is
the source of normal activities.

Some people dream of a world
in which there are no pigeons,
and this is a good world for dreamers,
but not a very good world for pigeons.

Sometimes a man
will point to a pussy
and is a man standing
and pointing to a pussy.

Women play a major role in the formation of pigeons.

Sometimes a man
will stand in a room
and the pussy will not
move very much.

Man is scrambling for
more resemblance to man
in the land of more resemblance
to pigeons.

There is no way to look at the pussy and not wonder what it is.

If it is clear what is happening
then it is clear there is a woman in
what is happening with the man standing
in what is happening with pigeons.

Act I, Scene I: Pussy.

Philosophy
really ought to
be written only
as a form of poetry
on pigeons.

A famous French painter
once painted a picture of pussy
and it was a very good likeness.
It was like the outside of the pussy.

You cannot touch a pigeon
without touching something
that normally refers to a pigeon.

Art and pussy never leave the world as it is.

In the absence
of all conversation
there is the distance
of all pigeons.

Sometimes there is
a great deal of pussy
in the areas of the world
where it seems like there
would be so little pussy.

Reality is not limited to these outings in the country.
The country is not limited to these outings in reality.
Reality is not limited to pigeons in general.

Some pussy emphasizes semantic density
over romantic intensity, but it is still pussy.

You cannot drop a
pigeon from a window
and expect that pigeon
to remain in a window.

I find James Joyce pretentious
but I find pussy really interesting.
It is interesting to think of James Joyce
as a normal man.

Pigeons are comfortable with the size of women.
Women are comfortable with the look of pigeons.

Sometimes you see
a woman's head and not
her pussy and sometimes you
see her pussy and not her head.

Some women have
a slightly surreal edge
which gives them roughly
the same edges as pigeons.

The eye of man
follows the pussy
with pious gloom.

There are more pigeons surrounding the river
than there is darkness surrounding the pigeons.

When my thoughts
turned to the darkness
of the river my thoughts
turned deeply to pussy.

Some pigeons revolve in
a constellation of revelatory images
and some pigeons fall just outside
the realm of revelatory images.

Darkness
is one of the
defining traits
of the interiority
of pussy.

In the case of
something beautiful
in the case of something
with pigeons.

Pussy is sometimes realistic
in the tradition of Flaubert
and sometimes quite dreamlike
in the tradition of women.

When I tell people
I write about pigeons
I tell people I write about
the large number of pigeons.

As I approached the pussy I was pleased
to find there were no aspens surrounding it,
just the warm contrast of two shades of orange.

Twelve feet away
in the form of a man
with a pigeon is the form
of a banal conundrum.

Sometimes there is an invocation for more pussy
and sometimes we are happy with the amount of pussy
we have.

The past is not particularly characterized
by ordinary language and the use of pigeons.

Transcendental pussy
has not alienated me
from ordinary pussy at all.

Some images of pigeons
are nonsensical and even
unnecessary as images but
very necessary as pigeons.

When I tell people
I write about pussy
I tell people I write about
both kinds of pussy.

Learn to recognize the shared practices
and actions of pigeons. Learn to recognize
the conditions under which they are pigeons.

Pussy can heighten
the poet's sense of absurdity
but it can also heighten
the poet's sense of familiarity.

The purpose of some pigeons
is to reenact the reality of pigeons
for the pigeons who no longer have
any toehold in reality.

The pussy and the face
are both on the front of a woman,
but the face is on the head,
and the head is very important.

Some men will not
stop to look at a pigeon
but they will stop to look at
a woman who feeds a pigeon.

I once saw pussy
in large block letters
on the front door of
a manufacturing plant.

Anything next to a pigeon
is next to a dream that jumps
from one pigeon to another.

I have been able
to read the pussy until
it read without any echo
of the regular world.

Women finally come to rest
on the equivalent of a pigeon.
The rest of the pigeon does not
happen in the image of a pigeon.

As the reality of pussy hangs
from the precipice of appearance,
the standers are standing and pointing
and the laughsters are laughing and laughing.

Pigeons occupy a marginal position in absurdity for men, but they occupy a central position in absurdity for pigeons.

I never laugh
when I see pussy
because pussy is not funny
and what is funny is not pussy.

An image
of a pigeon is
something of a prison
for a pigeon.

When I think of a woman
I think of more than just her pussy.
In the world of the great heart
the pussy is a fairly marginal figure.

One way
to look
at a pigeon
is a little.

I dream of a pussy that resounds
with all of the great features of reality, but
with all of the hallucinatory effects of nature.

Some fat kids are happy.
Some of all birds are pigeons.

How easy is it
to fall into
a world of pussy
with two different
vanishing points.

What used
to be a pigeon
is nothing at all
like what passes
for a pigeon now.

When she lifted her dress and showed me her pussy I became very interested in it.

There is indeed the inexpressible.
This shows itself; it is the pigeon.

Once a man
has seen a pussy
he will inevitably
try and talk about it.